SPECIALS

Penguin Specials fill a gap. Written by some of today's most exciting and insightful writers, they are short enough to be read in a single sitting – when you're stuck on a train; in your lunch hour; between dinner and bedtime. Specials can provide a thought-provoking opinion, a primer to bring you up to date, or a striking piece of fiction. They are concise, original and affordable.

To browse digital and print Penguin Specials titles, please refer to **www.penguin.com.au/penguinspecials**

From the Tsar's Railway to the Red Army:

The Experience of Chinese Labourers in Russia during the First World War and Bolshevik Revolution

MARK O'NEILL

PENGUIN BOOKS

Published by the Penguin Group
Penguin Group (Australia)
707 Collins Street, Melbourne, Victoria 3008, Australia
(a division of Penguin Australia Pty Ltd)
Penguin Group (USA) Inc.
375 Hudson Street, New York, New York 10014, USA
Penguin Group (Canada)
90 Eglinton Avenue East, Suite 700, Toronto, Canada ON M4P 2Y3
(a division of Penguin Canada Books Inc.)
Penguin Books Ltd
80 Strand, London WC2R 0RL, England
Penguin Ireland
25 St Stephen's Green, Dublin 2, Ireland
(a division of Penguin Books Ltd)
Penguin Books India Pvt Ltd
11 Community Centre, Panchsheel Park, New Delhi – 110 017, India
Penguin Group (NZ)
67 Apollo Drive, Rosedale, North Shore 0632, New Zealand
(a division of Penguin New Zealand Pty Ltd)
Penguin Books (South Africa) (Pty) Ltd
Rosebank Office Park, Block D, 181 Jan Smuts Avenue, Parktown North,
Johannesburg 2196, South Africa
Penguin (Beijing) Ltd
7F, Tower B, Jiaming Center, 27 East Third Ring Road North, Chaoyang
District, Beijing 100020, China

Penguin Books Ltd, Registered Offices: 80 Strand, London, WC2R 0RL,
England

First published by Penguin Group (Australia) in association with Penguin
(Beijing) Ltd, 2014

penguin.com.cn

ISBN: 9780734310477

CONTENTS

Into the Russian Darkness

'We worked twelve hours a day, cutting timber into strips and laying them on the track. We ate black bread and drank marsh water that had turned black. The Tsar's government cared nothing for the lives of Chinese. Those who were sick were forced to move logs and stones. Many people were driven to death in this way.'

Ji Shou-shan used these evocative words to describe his experience as a member of the construction gang that built a railway 1000 kilometres long, stretching from St Petersburg to the Arctic port of Murmansk. The work was carried out in the depths of winter, when there was no daylight for several months.

Ji was one of more than 200 000 Chinese workers who went to Russia during the Great War to assist in the Allied war effort. Some 135 000 Chinese men were also sent to France and Belgium between 1916 and 1922, but Russia would receive the majority of China's wartime labourers.

Despite assurances that they would not be involved in the war, thousands of Chinese workers dug trenches and carried ammunition for troops on the Eastern Front; many were captured and detained in German and Austrian prison camps. Others worked in farms, forests, factories and mines; built roads and railways; and loaded cargoes. The labourers were often cheated by the Chinese contractors who had hired them, and they did not receive the food, fuel and clothing they'd been promised.

Then, in 1917, life for the Chinese worsened when there were two revolutions in Russia – the overthrow of the Tsar and the Bolshevik seizure of power – followed by a civil war. The economy collapsed; many of the Chinese workers lost their jobs but could not return home because of the conflict. More than 40 000 Chinese workers joined the Red Army. Many of this number died fighting for the Revolution and are buried in unmarked graves all over the country. Some became bodyguards of Lenin and others joined the new Soviet secret police, the Cheka.

Stranded in a foreign land, thousands of kilometres from home and with no-one to help them, still others peddled goods on the street, begged or turned to crime.

Their plight has been described as the most tragic episode in 400 years of Chinese emigration. The men had crossed the border into Russia with dreams of earning enough money to build a house or business for their family at home. None could have imagined the hell that awaited them.

This book is the story of those 200 000 Chinese workers, a story that is scarcely known in Russia or China and rarely told elsewhere. Russian and Chinese history books describe the ferocious battles of the Great War, the October Revolution and the Civil War, but the Chinese workers are a mere detail in the corner of this huge canvas.

The workers' experience is as dramatic and extraordinary as that of the soldiers who were fighting beside them. They found themselves involuntary actors in a civil war that led to the establishment of the world's first Communist state and invasion by foreign armies from fourteen nations who wanted, in the words of Winston Churchill, to 'strangle the Bolshevik baby in its cradle'.

The New Masters
of the Land

The 200 000 Chinese workers who went to Russia during World War One represented the largest migration of Chinese to that country, but they were not the first.

Since the 1860s, over a period of more than fifty years, Chinese and Manchu had moved to the Russian Far East to join the small population that included Koreans, native people and ethnic Russians. The Chinese fished, hunted animals and dug for gold, ginseng and other roots in this vast territory; many were seasonal workers, arriving after the ice melted in the spring and staying until the start of winter.

The Russians had first reached the Pacific Ocean in 1639, during the conquest of the Siberian Khanate that added several million square kilometres of land to the Russian Empire's eastern borders. The empire grew larger still during the second half of the nineteenth century, the period of Russia's greatest expansion, extending to the Amur River on the border of China's northernmost province of Heilongjiang. Russia developed a strong military presence in the region, setting up naval outposts and encouraging its people to settle there.

Just to the south lay China, viewed by Russia and the other imperial powers as a plump chicken ripe for the taking. Between 1850 and 1864, the Qing government was embroiled in the Taiping Rebellion, one of the most deadly wars in history. The civil war in southern China took the lives of an estimated twenty million people, mostly civilians, and provided Russia with the perfect opportunity to exploit China's weakness and make legal its control over the Amur region.

Nikolay Muraviev, Governor-General of the Far East, camped tens of thousands of troops on the borders of Mongolia and Manchuria. His opportunity came as China was losing the Second Opium War (1856–60): when he threatened war on a second front, the Qing Dynasty agreed to enter negotiations with Russia.

Russia signed two very favourable agreements: the Treaty of Aigun in 1858 and the Treaty of Beijing in 1860. The treaties established a border between the two empires along the Amur River, south of the original border, and allowed Russia to begin building a port and naval base at Vladivostok. Under the Treaty of Aigun, the territory bounded on the west by the Ussuri River, on the north by the Amur and on the east and south by the Sea of Japan was to be jointly administered by Russia and China. Just two years later, in 1860, Russia gained sole control of this land and China lost more than one million square kilometres of territory.

The Qing emperor considered these treaties a time-saving measure before he dealt with the Russians more decisively. But the moment never came. When Moscow established the region of Primorsky Krai (Maritime Province), with Vladivostok as its administrative centre, China's access to the Sea of Japan was blocked.

Russia's new territory was expensive to govern, how-ever, and in 1867 the cost of developing and defending the Amur–Ussuri region led to the sale of Alaska to the United States for US$7.2 million.

Chinese labour on Russian land

Russia had acquired an enormous piece of territory, but it was forced to rely on Chinese labour to develop it. Few Russians wanted to move to the coldest and most remote part of the empire, despite the incentives that were offered, and the prisoners and political dissidents sent forcibly by the Tsar were not enough. Manpower was needed to build roads, railways, houses and facto-ries; to cut timber, dig for coal and iron ore; and to plant wheat, corn and vegetables in the fields.

From 1860 until 1882, there were no restrictions on foreigners entering the Russian Far East regions of

Primorsky and Amur. A survey taken in 1879 found that as many Koreans and Chinese were moving into the Maritime Province as Russians; for several years, the Chinese outnumbered the Russians. The Qing government encouraged the migration, as China's millions of unemployed were viewed as a potential source of trouble at home. Russian companies hired Chinese workers to build the new naval base and other public buildings in Vladivostok, and the migrants returned to China with money for their families and newly acquired skills.

In the 1880s, however, Russia began to be alarmed by the large influx of Chinese, and the term 'Yellow Peril' entered the vocabulary. The Russian government imposed a 'head tax' on Chinese migrants in 1887, and used the money raised to give incentives to Russians to settle in their place. In 1892, foreigners were banned from buying land. Despite these measures, migration from China continued; when gold was discovered in the Gilyuy River basin in the Amur region in 1896, thousands of Chinese travelled there, and beyond to the goldfields of Yakutsk. The opening of the Far East depended on Chinese labourers, and by 1910 they accounted for 81 per cent of foreign workers in the Amur and Primorsky regions employed in public works and gold mining.

The Chinese labourers also worked on the construction of Russia's railways. In March 1890, after visiting Japan, the future Tsar Nicholas II arrived in Vladivostok, where he blessed and inaugurated construction of the Far Eastern segment of the Trans-Siberian Railway, which would run 9259 kilometres to Moscow. 'I look forward to travelling in the comfort of the "Tsar's Train" across the unspoilt wilderness of Siberia,' he wrote in his diary. The train was designed and built in St Petersburg as a mobile office for the Tsar and his staff to travel across Russia.

Chinese manpower was essential to the realisation of this Pharaonic project, which bound the Russian Far East to European Russia; most of the non-Chinese workers were Russian prisoners. The Tsar hoped that the railway would accelerate colonisation of the Far East, just as the line to the Pacific had populated the western United States. He also wanted to move his soldiers quickly on the new line to face the Japanese who sought to control Korea and Manchuria. Conditions were harsh, especially during the winter when temperatures fell well below zero, and many Chinese workers died during the railway's construction. The stretch between Vladivostok and Khabarovsk was completed in 1897, and the line to Moscow in 1916.

Chinese workers were also the main labour force for the China Eastern Railway (CER), a short cut for the Trans-Siberian running from near the Siberian city of Chita through the north of Manchuria, via Harbin, to

Vladivostok. Traffic on the line started in November 1901. CER was a Russian company, with its headquarters in Harbin, capital of Heilongjiang province. Russian railway engineers preferred Chinese workers: they worked harder than the Russian workers and did not talk politics. They were also paid less: a government survey of the Maritime Province in 1911 found that the average monthly pay for a Russian was 58.27 rubles, compared to 38.08 rubles for a Chinese worker.

The railways not only brought Russians to the Far East; they enabled Chinese to reach Europe. On their morning promenade, the rich ladies of St Petersburg were astonished to find pedlars from China on the city streets, selling paper flowers and other items they had made; those who had nothing to sell turned to begging. Among the arrivals were better-funded migrants from Qingtian, Zhejiang province, who opened small shops and sold products from their hometown, such as flowerpots, carvings, handbags and other leather goods. The visitors were not popular and their begging created a negative image of the Chinese, who were badly treated by the police and public alike.

Massacre of the Chinese

One of the blackest episodes in Sino-Russian history occurred in 1900, when the Boxer Rebellion spread across northern China, targeting foreign missionaries and their Chinese followers. In June 1900, the Boxers laid siege to the foreign legation quarter in Beijing, which was defended by British, American, French, Italian and Russian troops. The rebellion spread as far north as Heihe, in Heilongjiang, and the Russian city of Blagoveshchensk on the opposite side of the Amur River. In July 1900, the Qing imperial army and Boxer rebels shelled Blagoveshchensk for almost two weeks.

The city's military governor and police chief decided to deport the entire Chinese community as potential fifth columnists. No-one was willing to provide boats to take the Chinese across the river to China, so they were taken to the river's narrowest point and pushed into the water. More than 3000 Chinese died, either drowning in the river or shot by Cossacks. The massacre would live long in the memory of Chinese residing in Russia; even today, no Chinese wants to live where it occurred, as it is believed that the spirits of the dead wander there still.

Thousands of Chinese living in Vladivostok, Khabarovsk and other centres were driven out of the country by the authorities, and the Russian Far East's Chinese population fell to its lowest level in fifty years. The government efforts to encourage internal migration were finally bearing fruit and the number of Russians surpassed those of Chinese. Primorsky's Russian population rose from 189000 in 1897 to 380000 in

1911, when the total population numbered 524 000; Amur's population of 286 000 in 1911 included 242 000 Russians, compared to 120 000 in 1897. Most of the migrants were farmers, a profession they continued in their new home, and the Chinese moved to the cities.

In 1910, the Chinese population in Primorsky and Amur was around 150 000, accounting for approximately 20 per cent of the two regions' population; only 5 per cent had a fixed residential property and 2 per cent had Russian nationality. The majority of Chinese migrants were young people with no permanent home; they arrived after the Spring Festival, stayed for between one and four years, or for as long as they could find work, and then went home. A minority were businesspeople who stayed for longer periods, opened shops and sold Chinese products.

Into European Russia

Following the outbreak of World War One, Chinese workers became an essential source of labour in many regions of Russia. With mass conscription, heavy casualties on the Eastern Front and hundreds of thousands of soldiers taken prisoner, Russia needed manpower. As they had done in Vladivostok and Khabarovsk, Chinese workers built roads and railways, mined coal, cut timber and dug the fields in European Russia.

The migration of the 200 000 Chinese workers during World War One followed the pattern set during the fifty years since the Treaty of Aigun and the establishment of the Russian Far East. During those years, some workers travelled with contracts approved by the Chinese government and visas approved by the Russian authorities; others went without contracts or visas, recruited by private companies or individuals, Chinese and Russian, who promised them a better life and an end to poverty.

Going to Work

The war on the Eastern Front began on 1 August 1914, with the Russian invasion of East Prussia and the Austro-Hungarian province of Galicia. The pre-war strength of the Russian army was 1.4 million men, with seventy infantry and twenty-four cavalry divisions; mobilisation added 3.1 million men, with millions more ready to fight.

Manpower aside, Russia was poorly equipped for war. Germany had ten times as much railway track per square kilometre; the Russian soldier travelled an average of 1290 kilometres to reach the front, the German soldier less than a quarter of that distance. Russia's heavy industry was too small to equip the enormous armies Tsar Nicholas wanted to raise, and her stock of munitions was limited. The country was blockaded by sea – German U-boats controlled the Baltic Sea, and Turkey, Germany's ally, controlled the Dardanelles, the entrance to the Black Sea. Russia also lost most of its foreign supplies and foreign exchange earnings with the outbreak of war. In 1913, the country exported 10 million tonnes of grain, more than 10 per cent of its harvest; one of the biggest export markets for its food was Germany.

Like other European leaders, Tsar Nicholas II did not expect the war to last long, and he was careful not to expose the fact that Russia was the weakest of the great powers. In 1914, 85 per cent of the Russian population were peasants living at a subsistence level, and the national literacy rate of those over the age of nine was 40 per cent. While the country grew enormous quantities of food, with grain accounting for 90 per cent of arable farming, it produced few manufactured goods and imported 70 per cent of its machinery; even agricultural implements such as axes, sickles and scythes were brought into the country. During the war, 20 per cent of its bullets, 40 per cent of its rifles and 60 per cent of its machine guns, airplanes and motor vehicles were imported. Russia borrowed US$4.5 billion, nearly all of it from Britain and France – a debt that the new Soviet government would repudiate in 1918; it was the largest default in history, and a major reason why the Western powers would oppose the new regime and try to overthrow it.

Despite the lack of armaments, the Russian high command ordered an immediate attack against East

Prussia. It was a catastrophe. Between 23 and 30 August 1914, at the Battle of Tannenberg in what is now Olsztyn in Poland, the German Eighth Army routed the Russian Second Army. More than 50 000 Russian soldiers were killed or wounded; 100 000 were taken prisoner and 500 guns were captured. Among the dead were some of Russia's best-trained officers.

The war in the east developed in a different way from that in the west, which turned into trench warfare over a limited area of northern France and western Belgium. In the east, the war was fought over a distance of more than 1600 kilometres, stretching from St Petersburg in the north to the Black Sea in the south, from the Baltic Sea in the west to Minsk in the east. The density of soldiers was lower and the lines were easier to break. Once a line was broken, the large distances and weak communication networks made it hard for the defender to bring reinforcements, which resulted in an enormous number of Russian soldiers being taken prisoner by the German and Austro-Hungarian forces. Historian Nik Cornish put the figure at five million, more than three times the total of 1.3 million British, French and German soldiers taken prisoner during the war.

A war of attrition set in on this vast Eastern Front. General Denikin, retreating from Galicia, wrote: 'The German heavy artillery swept away whole lines of trenches and their defenders with them. We hardly replied. There was nothing with which we could reply. Our regiments, although completely exhausted, were beating off one attack after another by bayonet . . . Blood flowed unendingly, the ranks became thinner and thinner. The number of graves multiplied.'

By the second year of the war, Russia was suffering a severe shortage of manpower. Total losses for the spring and summer of 1915 amounted to 1.4 million killed or wounded. On 5 August that year, the Russian army retreated and Warsaw fell to the German forces.

Unlike Britain and France, Russia did not have overseas colonies from which it could recruit soldiers and workers. Its western borders were closed by the war. There was only one country that had the number of men it needed and that could deliver them quickly – China. And Russia had fifty years of experience of just how useful those workers could be.

The model contract

Even as the war approached, the Russian government was aware that it would soon need thousands of additional workers. On 21 July 1914, a cabinet meeting discussed abolishing the restrictions on foreign labour. In August and November 1915, as Russian manpower continued to be decimated by the war, the government passed regulations to permit the entry of more Chinese workers.

Before 1914, the vast majority of Chinese workers had worked in the Far East. After the outbreak of war, labour shortages became so acute that they were sent all over the country, from Murmansk in the Arctic Circle to the trenches on the Eastern front, from the Donetz basin in the Ukraine to the fields of Siberia.

The demand for Chinese labourers began in earnest in 1916. That year, Liu Jingren, consul of the Chinese Embassy in Russia, proposed a contract with strict conditions: the men should have the same rights as Russian workers and the contract should state in detail the nature of the job, wages and living conditions; the men should not take part in work that contravened China's neutrality; and the Beijing government had the right to send people to supervise that these conditions were being met.

The contract included the following six main clauses:

1. Specify the work and the place – cutting timber, building roads or working in mines, for example – and the employer has no right to change the work or the place.

2. All workers must go through a medical examination and be taken by rail to their place of work. Each group should have 1000 men. The fare will be paid by the person who hires the men. Before they leave, they can take an advance, which they

can spend en route. Another sum will be in the hands of the hirer and the local government is to pay for repatriation.

3. Unskilled workers will receive lower pay than skilled craftsmen and technicians, who can earn up to double. In addition to pay, the workers will receive tools, winter clothes, wood to burn as fuel, and food customary to Chinese like rice, noodles, tobacco, liquor, cooking oil, sugar, tea and vegetables. Sometimes they will receive other kinds of foods at cheaper than market rates. The employer or hiring company should pay all fees, including transport, stamp tax and fees related to obtaining a passport. They will enjoy protection of Russian law, receive the same wages as their Russian colleagues, as well as accommodation, medical care, insurance and, if necessary, burial.

4. Working time is twelve hours a day, with a two-hour break in the middle. They will work seven days a week, except for Russian holidays and traditional Chinese holidays and ten to twenty days of holiday per year.

5. The men will work in groups of dozens or up to 100, under a contractor, and live in a tent with a cook, to be hired by the employer.

6. If a worker finds something illegal, he can approach the Chinese consulate or embassy, local

commercial committee or the Russian police. If he is lazy or disobedient, his employer can fine him or dock wages, but not more than 50 per cent of his daily wage. Some contracts also stated that, if a worker ran away and caused losses, he would be financially responsible; in order to prevent desertion, other contracts stated that the employer could hold some of the worker's wages or their passport.

This was the model contract drawn up in good faith by the officials of the Foreign Ministry in distant Beijing, eager to obtain the best treatment for their citizens who were going to assist their neighbour during the most devastating war in its history. It was a great improvement on the contracts given to Chinese workers who went abroad at the end of the Qing dynasty to work as indentured labourers in Peru, Cuba, South Africa and the United States, where conditions were little better than those of slavery.

Beijing supported the recruitment drive, provided that China's neutrality in the war was not contravened; it demanded that the workers did not serve on the front-line or perform war-related tasks. China was willing to help Russia as a member of the Allied coalition; it believed the Allies would win the war and that the workers in Russia, as in France and Belgium, would help to ensure China a place at the negotiating table after the victory.

The mountain is high, and the emperor is far away

But things did not turn out as the well-intentioned officials in Beijing designed and hoped. The 200 000 Chinese workers who went to Russia during World War One were less fortunate than their brothers who worked for the French and British.

The departure of labourers for France and Belgium was the result of negotiations between the Chinese government and Paris and London; Beijing was involved in drawing up the contracts and approved those which they signed. Workers who signed up for the British Chinese Labour Corps (CLC) received training and medical examinations at reception centres in Qingdao and Weihaiwei; they were given warm clothing and were well fed. After the men arrived in Europe, the three governments were responsible for supervising what happened to them. The workers were not entirely at the mercy of their superiors – army officers, sergeant majors and company managers – and had recourse to a higher authority if their contracts were not honoured and things went wrong.

It was a different story for the workers who went to Russia. The government in Beijing lost control of the recruiting. Its approval process was too slow, and many organisations, both public and private, were eager to profit from hiring the workers and sending them to Russia. The result was that many labourers travelled to Russia with contracts that had not been approved and did not contain the clauses specified by the Foreign Ministry; they found themselves in Russia with no legal protection and with no recourse in case of abuse. Many others travelled with no individual contract at all, but were accompanied by a Chinese middleman or contractor who signed the agreement on their behalf; the fate of these men was in the hands of the middlemen and the Russian employers.

Most of the workers took the train to the city of Harbin, capital of Heilongjiang province, where they boarded a train that took them west to the border town of Manzhouli. From there, they crossed into Siberia and a new life in a country they had never seen.

The main recruiter was Yicheng Company, ostensibly a civilian firm but in fact owned by Chinese and Russian officials and businesspeople, and largely staffed by civil servants. The company's founder was Zhou Mian, a senior official from Heilongjiang, and its chief executive was Chai Wei-tong, a senior official of Jilin province.

Yicheng had the widest reach of any recruiter. With its headquarters in Changchun, capital of Jilin province, it had offices all over the northeast and in cities in Shandong province, including Yantai and Qingdao, the main recruiting centre of Britain's CLC. The three provinces of Manchuria, as well as Hebei and Shandong, were full of unemployed or under-employed people eager to try their luck by working abroad; even those who had work were willing to apply, believing that life abroad had to be better than at home, where flooding and other natural disasters frequently occurred.

Yicheng was just one of many players in the market. Demand from Russia was so strong and the business so profitable that it attracted local governments and warlords as well as private companies. Middlemen such as these took their cut from the fees paid by the Russian employers, the cost of the passports, the bonuses for finding workers quickly and from agreements to buy clothes and food for them.

In theory, only the Foreign Ministry had the power to approve the contracts to be signed by the workers, with local governments issuing passports on their approval. In reality, passports were issued without the contracts being approved. The local governments also issued too many passports, more than the number of contracts and up to double in some places. Passports were issued from offices set up in the Russian Far East; later, the Russian authorities did not recognise these passports as valid, and treated those who held them as illegal workers. This led to many problems, including the level of wages and treatment given to the workers and the question of who would repatriate them at the end of their contract.

In addition to the men receiving contracts that had not been approved, many workers did not receive the food, clothing and other benefits they were due, as their contracts were vague about the obligations of the employer and contractor or omitted them all together. Some recruiters embezzled the clothes, food and other items that the workers should have received. For example, in 1916, Yicheng Company placed orders with local factories for 60 000 pieces of clothing on behalf of the workers. Instead of giving the clothing to the labourers, the company sold it on the black market.

The system was faulty and complicated, and the central government could not and did not supervise it properly. The new republic was only five years old, and its ability to control local governments was limited. A great deal of money was flowing into the pockets of local governments, warlords and private companies, and the orders and regulations sent from Beijing were ignored.

Over the next six years, this flawed system would have terrible, sometimes fatal, consequences for the workers.

The Chinese Worker Army

How many Chinese went to work in Russia during the war? Figures given by scholars vary widely. In his book *Chinese Workers in Russia and the October Revolution*, published in 1988, Li Yongchang put the total at around 450 000, including those who travelled with officially approved contracts and those who went without approval. He estimated 150 000 Chinese workers went to European Russia and 300 000 to Siberia and the Far East.

Most scholars, however, estimate the figure to be around 200 000. In a study published in 2010, one Russian scholar searched through the National Archives in St Petersburg. For the period between 1 January 1916 and 1 September 1917, he found records of 67 123 Chinese, of whom 23 450 worked in construction, 20 908 in railways, 3 127 in mining and 3 641 in factories, where they made steel, automobiles, textiles and other products. Thousands more were involved in cutting and moving timber. The peak month was July 1916, with 15 114 recruited, followed by March 1917 with 4937.

The workers were employed all over the country, from Murmansk and Karelia in the north to the Black Sea, Georgia and the Baku oilfields in the south; in Moscow and St Petersburg; in Belarus and the Ukraine. More than 65 000 went to work in European Russia.

According to the rules laid down by the Foreign Ministry in Beijing, the workers could not be employed at or near the front-line, as that would contravene China's neutrality in the war. However, according to an article published in January 2013 by Xie Qingming, a history professor at Jinan University, Guangzhou, 50 000 Chinese labourers did work at the front during the war – digging trenches, moving ammunition and doing other support work. Of this number, 20 000 were killed.

In an article in the Chinese magazine *World Military Affairs*, published in August 2013, Xu Jie put the death toll of Chinese on the front-line at more than 10 000. During a revolt against their bad treatment, a group of workers killed the seven Russian soldiers guarding them. In reprisal, the army sent in a large group of soldiers and killed all 300 of the rebellious Chinese.

Some Chinese workers were captured by the Germans, who put them to work in camps for prisoners of war. Conditions in the camps were poor and many died of overwork, disease or beatings.

The wide discrepancy in the figures reflects the scarcity of material on the workers. Many historical records in Russia were destroyed during the Revolution, and the wars and political campaigns of the last 100 years. In any case, most of the workers were illiterate and left no records.

For Chinese scholars, the subject has been difficult to research, as during the Soviet era they had limited or no access to Russian archives. Since 1991 and the breakup of the Soviet Union, access has improved.

For many years the story could not be told, as the reality did not correspond with the political line of the time. Examples of the maltreatment of Chinese at the hands of the Russian police and public, and the deaths of many from hunger and disease for lack of help, do not accord with commentaries about the 'historic friendship between the two great peoples'.

Railway to the Arctic

One of the first projects on which the Chinese were put to work was the construction of a railway line from the capital of St Petersburg to the new ice-free port of Murmansk, on the Kola Peninsula above the Arctic Circle. The rail link became a priority after the outbreak of war, when a sea and land blockade was imposed on

Russia by Germany and its allies.

Because of the blockade, Russia's allies, Britain and France, could send war materiel only via Norway and Sweden to the far northwest of Russia or to Vladivostok on the Pacific Ocean. The port of Arkhangelsk, on the White Sea in northern Russia, was also ice-free throughout the year, but it was further east than Murmansk and involved a longer journey from Europe. Vladivostok was thousands of kilometres from the front, and the Trans-Siberian Railway could carry only one-seventh of the supplies needed for the conduct of the war.

Washed by the Barents Sea in the north, and the White Sea in the east and southeast, almost all of the Kola Peninsula lies north of the Arctic Circle. Murmansk is close to the Gulf Stream, and experiences unusually high temperatures in winter; its excellent natural harbour provides protection against storms. However, the city has an annual average temperature of zero degree Celsius and sees daylight for only 300 days a year, with the polar night stretching from 22 November to 15 January. On average, it experiences 130 days of rain and 168 days of snow – more precipitation than any other city in Europe. The rail project had been discussed for thirty years but never built because of the enormous engineering difficulties posed by geography and climate.

Construction began on the first stretch of railway

in June 1914, running for 300 kilometres from St Petersburg to Petrozavodsk; it was finished in the summer of 1915. Preliminary surveys for the second stretch of 1044 kilometres, from Petrozavodsk to Murmansk, began in the autumn of 1914 and continued during the polar darkness, opening on 3 November 1916. The total cost was 180 million rubles. In order to build the railway in so short a time, the government hired 30000 peasants from all over Russia, and used the labour of more than 50000 German and Austrian prisoners of war, as well as about 10000 Chinese; in all, a total of 100000 people were involved in the construction.

The line was laid across frozen marshes, uninhabited rocky terrain, lakes, thick taiga and the permafrost of the Arctic tundra. The men worked in shifts twenty-four hours a day, through the cold and dark of winter when temperatures fell to minus 40 degrees. Many of the builders died due to the extreme conditions, lack of nutrition and disease; one estimate is 25000, or nineteen for every kilometre of railway line that was completed. Among the dead were 400 Chinese who died of cold; they did not receive the winter clothes promised under the terms of their contract.

One of the Chinese workers was Ji Shou-shan. In his memoirs, which were published in 1960, he wrote: 'We worked with German and Austrian PoWs in building the railway. The work was extremely heavy, cutting timber into strips and laying them below the track. We worked twelve hours a day, from seven in the morning until seven at night.

'Initially we ate steamed buns and later black bread and drank marsh water that had turned black. The diet had no fresh vegetables. We lived in log huts that were open to the wind on four sides. There were no doctors or medicines at the place of work. When I was recruited in China, I was told that I would receive 2 rubles a day. But, when I got here, I received only 30 rubles a month at most.

'The Tsar's government cared nothing for the lives of Chinese. Those who were sick were forced to move logs and stones. Many people were driven to death in this way.'

The Chinese workers earned half of the 3 to 4 rubles a day earned by the Russian workers. They were subject to abuse not only from the Russian guards but also from the German and Austrian prisoners.

Lifeline for war

The terrible sacrifice of the railway workers – Chinese, Russian, Austrian and German – proved invaluable for Russia during World War One, and during the war that followed between 1939 and 1945. The railway allowed the Russian navy to establish its Arctic flotilla at Murmansk, the last city founded in the Russian Empire. The settlement was named Romanov-on-

Murman on 6 July 1916, in honour of the family of the Tsar, and included a port and naval base. A year later, Murmansk had become the biggest city in the Kola Peninsula, with a population of around 100 000; there were seven moorages in the new port, able to serve ten large ships simultaneously and process the large quantities of war materiel sent by the British and French.

Chinese were among the first inhabitants of the new city, and the district of Shanghai was named after them. They ran bars serving a local brew called *hanzha*, and captains who needed sailors would do the rounds to pick up those who had passed out from drinking the potent concoction. The bars' unfortunate guests would wake up the next morning on a trawler heading out to sea.

Chinese workers were also sent to mine coal in the Donets Basin in the eastern Ukraine. Mining had begun there in the early nineteenth century, and by 1913 it produced 16.9 million tonnes of coal, more than 70 per cent of Russia's total output. Its mines are among the most hazardous in the world due to the enormous working depths, from 300 to 1 200 metres, along with high levels of methane, coal dust explosion and the danger of rocks bursting. The Chinese who laboured in the mines often lived entirely underground, close to their unenviable workplace.

Thousands more Chinese were employed in forests, cutting and moving timber and working in wood-processing factories. They lived in tents in the forest. One of them was Li Zhen-dong, who wrote in his memoirs: 'I was one of 12 000 poverty-stricken Chinese hired in 1916 at the height of the war. We worked in a forest not far from Petrograd. We were seeking a better life but were slaves to hardship. Working in Russia was like working in China. We had to work fifteen hours a day and slept in caves that were humid; they were crowded and dirty. We were paid very little, scarcely enough to feed ourselves.'

Yao Xincheng travelled from Dandong in Liaoning province with 200 others to work in a forest: 'We lived in a wooden hut. It was very frightening. We heard that, in the forest, there were wolves, lions, jackals and leopards. In addition, it was infested with many mosquitoes as big as dragonflies. Their bite was so painful that, even after an exhausting day at work, you could not sleep. We also had to protect ourselves from poisonous snakes. The air inside our hut was stale, like a pigsty.'

A Russian scholar described conditions in a forest in September 1916 in central Russia: 'Two thousand Chinese were working there but still had summer clothes. Some even had no shoes. In their tents, there was no heating equipment and water on the ground. They had received only a small portion of the flour, vegetables, cooking oil, sugar and potatoes to which they were entitled. So they went foraging or begging in villages nearby; the police beat them with batons and leather straps.'

Conditions worsen

Living conditions in Russia deteriorated as the war progressed, with severe shortages of food, clothing and other necessities. Relegated to the bottom of the social ladder, the Chinese workers earned only a survival wage and were the worst prepared for shortages and inflation.

The situation varied greatly across the enormous country. Most fortunate were those who worked in St Petersburg and Moscow; they had access to the Chinese Embassy and consulate, to which they could apply if they wished to change jobs, or report abuse or non-respect of their contract.

But this was not the case for the majority who worked in projects outside the cities and were at the mercy of their employers and the Chinese contractors who had hired them. According to the model contract drawn up by the Foreign Ministry in Beijing, the workers were supposed to receive clothing sufficient to endure the harsh Russian winter, be given food of sufficient quantity and quality to enable them to work properly, and fuel to provide warmth in the harsh winter. In reality, the employer and contractor kept a part of the food, clothing and fuel for themselves or to sell. Of the Chinese building the railway between Moscow and the Siberian district of Rybinsky, 107 died and 523 fell ill due to inadequate food, clothing and medical care.

The workers were also supposed to receive the same wages as the Russians with whom they were employed; this rule was often ignored and they received only 50 to 60 per cent of their wage, with the employer and contractor keeping the rest. In addition, the men often did not work at the place and in the job that they had been promised; those taken to the war's front-line were never told that this was their destination. They were sold from one contractor to another.

Workers who were dissatisfied with their conditions of work had no legal way to change jobs; the only alternative was to run away. When desertion became more prevalent, the Russian police became more strict; the Chinese labourers were forced to live apart from their Russian counterparts, in order to make them easier to control.

Another problem was the employer's refusal to repatriate the workers at the end of their term, as the contract specified. The Chinese workers had to make their own way home, and some did not have enough money to do so.

Strikes and protests

The Chinese workers vented their anger over their poor work and living conditions, primarily targeting the contractor who had hired them, and sometimes with violence.

Between 1915 and 1917, there were many protests. Some of the worst conditions were experienced in a mine in the Urals where 17 000 Chinese worked. In December 1915, the workers refused to go down into the pit and they destroyed the mine office. On 26 May 1916, a team of 2 600 Chinese working in a nearby timber factory, which was owned by the same boss, went on strike to protest at his refusal to improve their conditions and the arrest of their representative. The police were called and opened fire, killing one and injuring eight. The workers took up axes and stones and drove the police out; the local government summoned the army, who arrested 260 and threw them into jail.

A group of 580 workers hired by a Harbin contractor named Lin Qin to work in a forest in central Russia protested when, contrary to the contract they had signed, they received only half the wages of the Russian workers; they did not receive cash but food coupons. In winter, they did not have warm clothes; for food, they were given bread, boiled noodles and potatoes. On 21 September 1916, when they heard that their wages were to be reduced, 400 of the workers took axes, marched to the management office and demanded to see Lin Qin. Instead, they were met by Cossack police, whose commander ordered them to shoot; three were killed and forty-three seriously injured.

On 5 September 1916, a group of 517 Chinese working at a gold mine near Odessa marched to the company's management office carrying axes and wooden clubs, demanding clothes, wages and better food. After negotiations with local police and promises to deliver the clothes and wages, the workers returned to the mine. But their strike failed – the management did not deliver on its promises.

At the end of 1916, Chinese labourers working at a train station 90 kilometres from St Petersburg went on strike. To end the strike, police killed ten and put forty in prison.

Anger at home

The workers sent petitions and complaints to the Chinese Embassy in St Petersburg, which forwarded them to Harbin, where most of the contracts had been signed. The government office there informed the recruiters of the demands of the Ministry of Foreign Affairs: improve the conditions of work, do not let the men work in danger near the front-line and allow Chinese officials to visit the workers.

Liu Jingren, the consul in St Petersburg responsible for this dossier, told his government to slow down the recruiting. From early 1916, he sent reports to the Foreign Ministry in Beijing of workers being sent to the front to dig trenches; he stated that contracts were not being honoured, and described the workers' exploitation and maltreatment.

As news of the workers' bad treatment spread, the German Embassy and consulates in China disseminated the reports through their information channels. In response, the Chinese government slowed down the issue of passports and adopted a less positive attitude towards the recruiting. In January 1917, the German Foreign Ministry protested to Beijing and demanded a total ban on recruitment, accusing China of aiding enemy countries. To Germany, the recruitment policy was seen as little different from sending soldiers to fight on the Allied side.

For the Chinese workers in Russia, their conditions were akin to slavery: they had no rights, they were sent to work on the war front, they were moved from one job to another, and they were sold on by the contractors – all illegal practices.

From Tsar to Bolshevik Revolution

As 1916 rolled into 1917, the Chinese workers in Russia became caught up in the dramatic events that were unfolding around them, events that would lead to an outcome that would affect them profoundly.

The declaration of war in 1914 had initially produced an outburst of patriotic fervour and support for Tsar Nicholas II, but this dissipated when his people saw the results at the battlefront. By the end of that year, just five months into the war, 390 000 Russians had been killed and nearly one million injured. Far sooner than expected, recruits who had been barely trained were called up for active duty.

The Russian army achieved initial successes against the Austro-Hungarian forces allied to Germany and conquered large areas of Galicia, in western Ukraine. But the situation changed in 1915, when Germany shifted the focus of attack to the Eastern Front. The German army was better led, better supplied and better trained, and it drove the Russian army out of Galicia and Russian Poland. By the end of October 1916, Russia had lost between 1.6 and 1.8 million soldiers, with two million taken prisoner and one million missing.

The war's effect on Russia's economy was equally devastating, exposing the huge gulf between the two powers' industrial capacity. With German naval vessels and submarines holding the Baltic Sea and the Ottoman Empire controlling access to the Black Sea, Russia's ports were limited to Murmansk and Arkhangelsk on the Arctic Ocean and Vladivostok on the Pacific. The Russian army was running short of ammunition, uniforms, food and even shoes. By mid-1915, men were being sent to the front without arms – they were told to use weapons recovered from fallen soldiers from either side.

The internal transport system was monopolised by the military and could not deliver the food and daily necessities required by Russia's cities and industrial workers. By the end of 1915, there were food shortages and inflated food and fuel prices. In St Petersburg, the price of flour rose by 99 per cent between 1913 and 1916; meat rose by 232 per cent, butter by 124 per cent and salt by 483 per cent. The early loss of the coalfields in Poland meant a shortage of coal and a flood of two to three million refugees into Russia; in 1917, this number grew to 9.7 million, all of whom needed to be fed.

By 1917, prices were up to four times higher than

they had been in 1914. The profits did not go to farmers but to the middlemen who bought their food, so the farmers tended to hoard their grain and revert to subsistence farming.

St Petersburg was at the end of a long supply line. Shops closed early for lack of bread, sugar, meat and other provisions; lines lengthened for what remained. Working-class women spent forty hours a week waiting in food queues; to earn a living, they turned to begging, prostitution and crime.

Opposition to the war

Increasingly, the Russian people asked themselves for what purpose and for whom they were fighting this terrible war, but the absolutist system of government blocked the resolution of many urgent problems.

Tsar Nicholas II was an autocrat who believed in his divine right to rule; he was convinced that whatever their sacrifices, the loyalty of the Russian people was unshakeable. A famous photograph taken in 1914 shows the Tsar on a horse holding a religious relic in front of kneeling soldiers; the image captures exactly the mix of religious and royal power in which he believed.

In the autumn of 1915, Tsar Nicholas II went to the front to take over leadership of the army himself, leaving the government in the hands of his German-born wife, Alexandra, and the Duma (Parliament). Alexandra was deeply unpopular; not only was she half-German and completely unqualified to conduct an industrial war against the world's most powerful military power, one of her closest advisers was a mystic named Grigori Rasputin. Alexandra came to believe that God was speaking to her though Rasputin and that he was the only person who could save her only son, Alexei, who suffered from haemophilia.

Rasputin's influence over the Tsarina increased after the Tsar went to the front. The mystic was loathed by the political class and by the Russian Orthodox Church, and on 30 December 1916, a group of noblemen shot him and dumped his body in the Neva River.

As the death toll on the front increased and living conditions at home deteriorated, discontent became widespread among three key groups: the farmers, the workers and the soldiers. Land ownership was highly concentrated in Russia, with 1.5 per cent of the population owning 25 per cent of the land. Most farmers were tenants who barely survived, for whom inflation and the disruption of transportation during the war made conditions even worse.

Industrialisation had come late to Russia, and the factory workforce was highly concentrated: in 1914, around 40 per cent of industrial workers were employed in factories with more than 1 000 people; the figure in the United States was 18 per cent. In Moscow and St Petersburg, there were strong trade unions and Socialist movements; everyone remembered the Bloody Sunday massacre of January 1905, in which the Tsar's troops shot hundreds of unarmed protestors. In response, workers launched a crippling general strike, which forced Nicholas II to allow an elected Parliament.

By 1916, many of the officer corps who had grown up in loyalty to the Tsar had been killed and been replaced by soldiers who had risen through the ranks and had no such unquestioning obedience. When they saw the enormous numbers of men killed and taken prisoner, and the inept strategies of their superiors, the soldiers asked what they were fighting for. Were they simply cannon fodder to serve the interests of the rich and powerful?

In October 1916, the St Petersburg branch of the secret police, the Okhrana, warned of 'the possibility in the near future of riots by the lower classes of the empire enraged by the burdens of daily existence'. In November of that year, the State Duma warned the Tsar that unless a constitutional form of government was put in place, a terrible disaster would grip the country.

The problems were very clear, but Nicholas II chose to ignore the advice being given to him.

Overthrow of the Tsar

At the beginning of February 1917, workers in St Petersburg – which was now known as Petrograd, the Russian version of the name – began strikes and demonstrations. On 7 March, workers at Putilov, the city's largest industrial plant, announced a strike; it produced artillery for the army and railway rolling stock.

The next day, a series of meetings and rallies were held for International Women's Day, which turned into economic and political gatherings. Demonstrators demanding bread were supported by the industrial workers, who considered them a reason for continuing the strikes. The women workers marched to nearby factories, bringing out over 50 000 workers on strike. By 10 March, they had shut down virtually every industrial firm in the capital, as well as many commercial and service enterprises. Students, white-collar workers and teachers joined the workers in the streets and at public meetings. Several thousand Chinese workers lived in the city, and their sympathies lay with the strikers.

To quell the riots, the Tsar turned to the army. At least 180 000 troops were available in the capital, but most were either untrained or injured. Of these, only about 12 000 could be regarded as reliable, and they were reluctant to move against the crowd, since it included many women. In January 1905, the soldiers had been willing to fire on protesting workers, but not this time: on 11 March, when the Tsar ordered the army to suppress the rioting by force, troops began to mutiny.

Some soldiers joined the rioting and many officers were either shot or went into hiding; the army had lost its ability to put down the protests. People tore down symbols of the Tsarist regime all over the capital and the government's authority collapsed.

The response of the Duma, urged on by the liberal bloc, was to establish a Temporary Committee to restore law and order. Meanwhile, on 12 March, the socialist parties established the Petrograd Soviet to represent the city's workers and soldiers. The remaining loyal units switched allegiance the next day.

On 14 March, the Tsar took a train back towards Petrograd; it was stopped by a group of disloyal troops. When he finally reached his destination, the Army Chiefs and his remaining ministers suggested unanimously that he abdicate. He did so the next day on behalf of himself and his son; he nominated his brother, the Grand Duke Michael Alexandrovich, to succeed him.

Six days later, Nicholas, no longer Tsar and addressed with contempt by the sentries as 'Nicholas Romanov', was reunited with his family and placed under house arrest by the newly formed Provisional Government. It was the end of the dynasty that had ruled Russia since 1613.

The Provisional Government

The Provisional Government took over from the Tsarist regime on 15 March. The new government was recognised nine days later by Britain, France and Italy, which insisted that it continue to fight the Germans on the Eastern Front. The Allies wanted to avoid a peace settlement or surrender in the east at all costs, as it would enable the German army to move hundreds of thousands of soldiers to the front in France and Belgium.

On 18 April, the Minister of Foreign Affairs Pavel Milyukov sent a note to the Allied governments, promising to continue the war to 'its glorious conclusion'. In response, on 20 and 21 April, workers and soldiers held massive demonstrations against the continuation of war, and demanded the resignation of Milyukov.

The Provisional Government was unable to make decisive policy decisions due to political factionalism and a breakdown of state structures. Much of the real power rested in the hands of its rival, the Petrograd Soviet, which was especially strong in the army and the railways.

The Bolshevik Party was also increasing its influence in the city, in part because of its well-organised militia; by September 1917, it had gained a majority in the Petrograd Soviet, with Trotsky as chairman. The party advocated an end to the war and the enormous number of casualties, even if it meant surrender to the

Germans and the loss of territory. Vladimir Lenin, the party's leader, believed that Russia was fighting the war as a tool of French and British capitalist imperialism and that an end to the war was essential to consolidate Soviet power at home, a position that was extremely popular among the soldiers and urban workers. Bolshevik members spread this message in the army, creating disaffection and a sense of mutiny.

The Provisional Government further weakened the authority of the officer class by setting up 'soldier committees', which took over many of the powers formerly reserved for officers; it also abolished the death penalty in the army. Discipline in the army was weakened, and riots and mutinies became widespread. Officers were often the victims of harassment and even murder by the soldiers.

Despite the deteriorating condition of his army, Alexander Kerensky, the Minister of War, ordered an offensive in July 1917. It proved to be the last by the Russian army during the war. Kerensky hoped that an important Russian victory would gain popular favour and restore the soldiers' morale; this in turn would strengthen the weak government and prove the effectiveness of 'the most democratic army in the world', as he called it.

Starting on 1 July 1917, the Russian troops attacked the German and Austro-Hungarian forces in Galicia, pushing toward Lviv. Initial Russian success was the result of powerful bombardment, never witnessed before on the Russian front; most of the artillery came from Britain and Japan. The Austrians could not resist this bombardment, and the broad gap in the enemy lines allowed the Russians to advance without encountering any resistance. But the German forces proved much tougher, and their stubborn defence resulted in heavy casualties amongst the attacking Russians.

As Russian losses mounted, the infantry became increasingly demoralised; further successes were due to the work of cavalry, artillery and special 'shock' battalions, as most of the other soldiers refused to obey orders. By 16 July, the Russian advance had collapsed altogether. On 19 July, the Germans and Austro-Hungarians counterattacked, meeting little resistance. Next day, the Russian lines were broken, and by 23 July the Russians had retreated 240 kilometres. On 3 September, German troops entered Riga, one of the largest cities in the Russian Empire. The Russian troops defending the city refused to fight and fled. In October, the Germans carried out amphibious landings on Estonian islands. These operations brought German forces to within less than 500 kilometres of Petrograd, adding to the chaotic political situation in the city.

The military rout greatly weakened the Russian Provisional Government and increased the possibility of a Bolshevik coup d'etat. The failed offensive revealed the extent of poor morale within the army; no Russian general could now count on the soldiers under his command to do what he ordered.

The rise of the Bolsheviks

Conditions were now ripe for Lenin and his party to make their final move. On 25–26 October, Red Guard forces under the leadership of Bolshevik commanders launched their final attack on the ineffectual Provisional Government. Most government offices were occupied and controlled by Bolshevik soldiers on 25 October. The last holdout of the Provisional Ministers, the Tsar's Winter Palace on the bank of the Neva, was captured on the night of 26 October.

The Bolsheviks replaced the government with their own. They abolished private property, nationalised Russian banks and repudiated 13 billion rubles in Allied war loans paid to the Tsar.

The Allies refused to recognise the new government, which the press described as 'the enthronement of anarchy at Petrograd'. In December 1917, the Allied Supreme War Council pledged support to Russian forces that were committed to a continuation of war against Germany. But the new regime did not wish to continue the war against the Germans, and on 3 March 1918 the new Soviet republic signed the Treaty of Brest-Litovsk with Germany, ending the war on the Eastern Front.

It was a humiliation for Russia. The country lost one-quarter of the former Russian Empire's population and industry, including 90 per cent of its coalmines. It renounced all territorial claims to Finland, Belarus and Ukraine, and the three Baltic states of Estonia, Latvia and Lithuania. Poland became an independent state.

The driving force behind the signing of the treaty was Lenin. Despite the enormous losses, he believed that only an immediate peace would allow the young Bolshevik government to consolidate power in Russia, against all its enemies. He also considered the enormous number of casualties.

In his book *The Russian Army and the First World War*, historian Nik Cornish put the number of military dead at 2.006 million, 5 per cent of the male population between the ages of fifteen and forty-nine. Cornish estimated that the number of civilian casualties in Russia may have reached as high as 1.5 million. The treaty meant that the five million prisoners of war could go home – including many Chinese workers who had been working with Russian military units and been captured.

The Fate of the Chinese Workers

Following the Revolution, during the rule of the Provisional Government, many of the factories, mines and companies employing Chinese workers closed or went bankrupt. They could not or would not fulfil one of the most important clauses in the contract the workers should have signed – repatriating them to China at their expense. Thousands of Chinese found themselves without work or shelter, and with no-one to take responsibility for them.

Before the Revolution, the workers had earned an average wage of 30 rubles a month, enough to survive during the time of relative price stability. They had little savings and prices were continuing to rise. Many did not have the money or means to obtain a railway ticket back to China, and were driven to begging or crime to survive and earn the money needed to return home.

Those who could not return went to the big cities, where they worked as traders in street markets, did odd jobs or survived as vagrants. The flood of Chinese into Petrograd had been considered an issue for some time. On 24 April 1917, officials of the Interior Ministry and representatives of the Chinese Embassy had held a meeting on the issue. Rather than increasing allowances for jobless Chinese, which would invite more arrivals, the officials decided to try to improve the job conditions and rights of the temporary workers. On the issue of repatriation, the meeting set up a special committee, with the involvement of the Chinese Embassy. It arranged for Chinese and Russian officials to see where the workers lived, provide financial help to those who were sick and without funds, and arrange for travel home at reduced prices or free of charge. Thanks to this initiative, several thousand Chinese had returned to China by September 1917.

Beijing then went further and asked the Provisional Government to repatriate all the workers; it refused. When Beijing asked that the government repatriate those with legal contracts, the Provisional Government countered by saying that many of the workers had already returned home, while others had died: as for the rest, it needed to verify those who were legal and those who were not, as it did not have the money to organise a large-scale repatriation.

While the Provisional Government was more sympathetic to the plight of the Chinese workers than the Tsarist regime, it did not implement an effective repatriation policy. It was a critical moment in Russia's history: the country was still at war, facing the most powerful military nation on earth, which held millions of its citizens as prisoners of war. Repatriating foreign workers, many of them considered to be in the country illegally, was not a priority.

In response, the workers set up their own small groups to try to find a way home. Some managed to complete the journey; others were robbed and killed en route, died of cold or hunger, or, in despair, took their own lives.

Union of Chinese Workers in Russia

On 14 March 1917, China cut diplomatic relations with Germany, and on 14 August it entered the war on the Allied side. The United States had joined the Allies in April that year, making a victory by the Allied coalition virtually certain. Beijing wanted to be on the winning side, and gain benefits from the peace settlement that followed the war.

China's decision did nothing to help its thousands of citizens on the streets of Petrograd, Moscow and Omsk in their daily lives or in their quest to go home, but on 18 April 1917, in the midst of the chaos and misery, came a piece of good news – the formation of an association to help the workers. The Union of Chinese

Workers in Russia (UCWR) was established by a group of eight Chinese students in Russia, who registered the union in Petrograd. It was the first association of Chinese in Russia.

The association's chairman was a secondary school mathematics teacher named Liu Zerong. A native of Guangzhou, in 1897 five-year-old Liu had gone with his parents to live in the Caucasus, where his father had been invited to teach tea cultivation. Liu was schooled in Russia, and before the Revolution he was studying architectural engineering at St Petersburg University. He then worked as a teacher of mathematics in a middle school. His Chinese students were moved by the suffering of their compatriots, and wanting to do something to help, especially to facilitate their return home, they established the union, with the slogan 'raise wages, equal treatment, help those who have run away and arrange repatriation'.

The association included Chinese diplomats and businesspeople as well as students. Some members gave up their well-paid jobs or studies to care for the Chinese workers and to lobby for them with the government. The government in Beijing sent a grant of 100 000 rubles to help the workers, who received only one-third of the funds, the remainder being kept by China's embassy in Petrograd. Over the next twelve months, however, the embassy would help 30 000 workers return home.

The embassy also helped jobless Chinese find new employment, setting up recruiting offices and contacting Russian factories that needed workers. It lobbied for them to receive the same wages and benefits as Russian workers, and set up centres for the workers to help them obtain medical treatment and accommodation.

When the Bolsheviks seized power in October 1917, there were nearly 200 000 Chinese in Russia, the majority of whom welcomed the new government.

Liu Fu, who was working on the railway, recalled: 'After we heard of the October Revolution, I and my Russian colleagues were all extremely happy. I helped them put up the red flags with hammer and sickle over the railway station. We shouted our support for the new government and the overthrow of the Kerensky regime. We began to understand a truth that we did not know – poor people can take power in their country, instead of having to search everywhere for a reasonable life and happiness.'

The Chinese workers in Russia belonged to the lowest class of society – urban and rural workers with no secure job or income and no civil rights. Russians looked down on them; they were an easy target for harassment and robbery by the police and local militia. The ideology of the Bolsheviks – rule on behalf of the proletariat and the equality of workers around the world – was very appealing. Life under the new government had to be better than what they had experienced before.

For their part, the Bolsheviks wanted to gain the support of the Chinese workers. The country was bitterly divided between different classes, parties and regions; the new government needed all the help it could get.

Chinese join the Red Army

The terms of the Brest-Litovsk treaty enraged Russia's former Allies; it meant that Germany could move thousands of soldiers to the Western Front and recover thousands of tonnes of war materiel the Allies had sent to Russia. They were also enraged at the repudiation of the debts owed to them, and terrified that the new Soviet government would export its philosophy of violent revolution to the workers and soldiers of their own countries.

The Allies resolved to support those fighting the Bolsheviks in the civil war that had erupted to overthrow the new regime. In Russia, the new government was opposed by dozens of groups, including landowners, republicans, conservatives, much of the middle class, pro-monarchists, liberals, army generals, non-Bolshevik socialists and democratic reformists. Their military forces, known as White Russian armies, were led by generals of the Tsarist army, who controlled large parts of the empire. They were helped by armies from fourteen Allied countries, in a civil war that would last for five years and cost at least 3.7 million casualties.

The civil war did not directly involve Chinese workers; they were outsiders in a domestic conflict. Nonetheless, thousands of Chinese joined the Red Army and fought with bravery and distinction on many fronts, including Poland, Belarus, Ukraine, the Caucasus, the Volga region and Siberia.

Russian and Chinese scholars' estimates of the number of Chinese Red Army soldiers differ; the consensus is 40 000 to 50 000. Some estimates, including those of Chinese Foreign Ministry diplomats at the time, reach 70 000. An article in the *Shen Bao* newspaper of September 1921 reported that a figure of 60 000 Chinese in the Red Army was too conservative: 'between 1917 and 1922, there were at least 200 000 Chinese in the Soviet Union. In addition to those in the regular army, many others joined local militia or fought as guerillas.'

The Chinese wore the same uniform as other soldiers in the Red Army. They fought under Russian officers, who found them determined and efficient. Most had a limited understanding of Russian, which meant that they had no attachment to Russian personalities or places and were insulated from outside influences; their officers could use them to commit executions.

They were also useful as 'shock troops' because the enemy did not expect an attack by people of a different ethnicity.

The Chinese presence was used in the propaganda of the White Russian side as evidence that, because it used Chinese, Latvians and other foreigners, the Red Army did not have the support of the Russian people.

The Chinese were fighting against the will of their own government, as together with other Allied countries, Beijing did not recognise the Soviet regime. In 1918, the Beijing government sent naval vessels and soldiers into the Russian Far East to protect the lives and property of Chinese residents there. It was part of an Allied force of 90 000 soldiers in Siberia that intervened to support the White Russian armies.

So why did so many Chinese risk their lives to fight for a foreign government? Some were inspired by the ideals of the Revolution that promised a better future for the poor and under-privileged. The Bolshevik Party excelled at spreading this message, and published a Chinese-language newspaper called *The Greatness of Equality* in order to reach this group of forgotten and marginalised people. Lenin was rare among Russian leaders in having an international outlook; he was favourable to Chinese and welcomed them into his party, treating them in a way that was very different from the vast majority of Russians.

White Russian soldiers treated Chinese as suspects, likely to be Bolshevik spies. On 28 March 1919, the political newspaper *Pravda* reported that White Russian soldiers in the south of the country had beaten to death fifty Chinese from Hubei and Shandong, including eleven women and twenty-three children, for no apparent reason.

While some Chinese volunteered for reasons of ideology, the majority joined up because it offered an escape from a life of misery and hopelessness. Becoming a soldier meant proper clothing, regular meals and warm accommodation. It gave them social status and respect they had never enjoyed before in Russia.

Others joined because they were forced to. Desperate for more men, both sides in the civil war used violence to make people join their ranks. The choice was sign up or be executed.

China's first Bolshevik

The most famous and highest ranking Chinese in the Red Army was Ren Fuchen, aged thirty-three at the time of the Revolution and considered China's first Bolshevik.

Ren was commander of the Chinese Red Eagle battalion when he was killed in November 1918. In November 1989, the Soviet Union gave him a Red Flag medal of honour; a statue of Ren was erected in 1993 in his home town of Tieling, Liaoning province, proclaiming him to be a 'hero of the proletariat'.

Ren was born in April 1884 in a rural district of Tieling. Since his family was poor, he had only five years of formal schooling while he lived with an uncle who was a teacher. As family circumstances improved, he entered a college in Tieling. In 1898, he joined a Russian company that was building the railway from Harbin to the port city of Dalian, as a secretary; it was during this time that he began to study Russian.

In 1904, with the outbreak of the Russo-Japanese war, he was attached to the Russian army as an interpreter. He learnt of the Social Democratic Workers Party, the forerunner of the Bolshevik Party, as many of the officers he met were members. Inspired by them, he gave up a secure job as a policeman and moved to a Russian army school in Harbin, to teach Chinese.

In 1908, Ren secretly joined the Bolshevik Party, making him the first Chinese to become a member. He managed to avoid arrest by the Tsarist secret police, but was shot and badly wounded by a Chinese in their pay. While he was recovering in hospital, the secret police planned to finish him off. His wife, Zhang Hanguang, managed to smuggle him out in disguise, and with the aid of party members, he escaped by night to Qiqihar. He returned to the police force, working at the head of a patrol on the border with China; the mission the Party gave him was to help its members who had been sent as prisoners to Siberia to escape into China.

The Tsarist government demanded his extradition, but Ren's connections with the local government protected him and enabled him to remain employed in China.

In December 1914, Ren signed up as one of 2000 Chinese to go to the Perm district in the Urals, to work in mining and timber. One year later, his wife and three children came to join him. Living conditions for Ren and his fellow workers were terrible. They were under-fed and did not receive proper medical care; some fell ill and died. Ren campaigned actively for better condi-tions and won the support of his fellow workers. He set up a revolutionary cell, and in 1916, when the mine owners held back some of their wages, he organised a strike. The owners informed the local police, who put him under house arrest for 'organised violence'. Thanks to the help of prominent Chinese businessmen, Ren was released and working conditions improved. This success stiffened the resolve of the workers.

In November 1917, when news of the Revolution reached the Chinese workers in Perm, they were over-joyed and rushed to spread the good news. Under Ren's leadership, all of them went to join the Red Army. A Chinese unit was set up immediately to defend the new regime against its domestic and foreign enemies. Ren purchased rifles and ammunition, and on 25 November 1917, in the Kama mining region of the Upper Volga, he organised the first Chinese armed unit of the Red Army. His actions caught the eye of Lenin, who ordered that Ren be appointed brigade commander.

The Chinese were warmly welcomed by the Red Army and put into the Third Army as the 29th Strike Brigade; Ren became political commissar. After a short period of training, they were sent to the front.

The end of 1917 was the most difficult period for the new government, especially on the Eastern Front, where the White Russians had the support of the Allied powers. The Chinese brigade went into battle in a village near the mining district and wiped out the enemy.

In the spring of 1918, the Chinese brigade fought in the area of the Kama River in the Volga region; the brigade fought well and earned the praise of their superiors for their dedication and spirit, but the death toll was high, with up to half of the men dying. Ren was diligent in teaching his men Communist philosophy, telling his men: 'If you do not want to die for the sake of Russians, remember that, since you were young, you have seen Chinese killed at the hands of Russians and Japanese. Today you are fighting to the death for the first government of farmers and workers.'

In October 1918, the brigade was successfully fighting followers of White Russian General Alexander

Kolchak, killing and wounding several hundred and capturing 300. On 27 October, the Supreme Soviet named the brigade the Red Eagle battalion and presented the flag at a ceremony in a nearby town. Russian soldiers shouted at the ceremony, 'Real friends.'

One night in late November, Ren's brigade was sleeping in a railway car; it was isolated, against a much larger force of White Russians. Ren thought it might be his last battle and told an aide that, if he died, he wanted to leave everything to his wife. An informer gave the White Russians the precise location of the railway car, and they attacked it with machine guns. The battle lasted several days and nights, and the brigade received no support. The next day a detachment of the Red Army arrived and discovered that Ren and all his men had been killed.

On 28 December, a Communist newspaper published Ren's obituary, written by the Soviet government: it greatly praised his spirit, saying that he had given his effort and trust to the Soviet state: 'This revolutionary fighter will live on forever as a son of the Chinese people who gave his life for the oppressed people of the world.'

Lenin's bodyguard

Another famous Chinese in the Red Army was Li Fuqing, who became one of the personal bodyguards of Vladimir Lenin.

Li was born in 1898 into a poor family in Shenyang; his father was a carpenter. To help the family, Li began raising pigs and cattle at the age of thirteen. He then became a coal miner and in April 1916 learnt that a Russian company was offering payment of 200 rubles for a two-year contract. Along with his two cousins, he joined a group of 3 000 Chinese travelling by train from Harbin across the border into Russia.

The men were told that they would be working in a factory, but after many days' travel they were ordered to leave the train. They found that they were in a forest and there was no factory. Their job was to build trenches close to the front. They were roughly treated by the Tsarist soldiers, who beat them with rifles and leather straps. Unable to bear this treatment, one worker hung himself and another cut off his own fingers.

Soon after, Li, his colleagues and Tsarist guards were taken prisoner by the Germans and put in a camp, where they built roads and prisons; their diet was just a few pieces of black bread. In the spring of 1917, for reasons Li did not understand, the Chinese men and soldiers were released and made their way back to Russia.

While they were crossing the plains of Ukraine, a Russian appeared and told them that they would die of hunger unless they organised themselves and attacked a nearby Tsarist army depot supplied with food, clothes and weapons. Li knew enough Russian to understand. He and 180 Chinese joined 300 Russians, who had brought weapons from the battlefield; they attacked a police station in a small town and took thirty rifles. Later, they attacked an army base and seized nearly 100 rifles. So a revolutionary brigade was formed.

During its guerilla activities, the Chinese and Russians formed warm relations, sharing the little they had. This friendship was nothing like the workers had experienced before. Shortly afterwards, Li and the other Chinese joined the Red Army. His brigade saw action in Belarus, Ukraine, the Upper Volga and Poland.

In the winter of 1918, Li was chosen as one of 200 soldiers, including seventy Chinese, to serve as body-guards of Vladimir Lenin. He was in a group of four that stood guard below his office and accompanied him when he went outside. Lenin sometimes spoke to them. Aged only twenty and illiterate, Li did not understand Russian well.

In October 1919, Li was sent to the Ukraine as a squadron commander in a cavalry regiment to fight a White Russian army. He did not see Lenin again. In January 1924, when Lenin died, Li was studying at a military academy in Moscow; he was sent to the funeral as a representative of the students.

In 1931, Li was sent to Xinjiang, where he was put under house arrest by a local warlord. Not allowed to leave the region, he opened a restaurant in Urumqi, the provincial capital. In 1949, when the People's Liberation Army captured Xinjiang, he enrolled as a chef, at the age of fifty-one. In 1957, he was invited to Moscow to attend the fortieth anniversary of the October Revolution.

Iona Yakir

Chinese volunteers also fought in a regiment of the Red Army led by Iona Yakir, one of its most famous commanders. In early 1918, Yakir's Chinese regiment fought in the Ukraine against occupation forces of the Austro-Hungarian army; its men fought with bravery and determination.

Yakir went on to become one of the top commanders of the Red Army during the civil war and received the Order of the Red Banner three times. After studying at the Higher Military Academy in Berlin in 1928 and 1929, he reformed the Red Army. In 1936, he conducted military manoeuvres near Kiev involving 65 000 troops, including tanks and aircraft. The exercises were the largest ever conducted in the world and amazed the military representatives of the Western powers who witnessed them.

Suspicious of such innovation and independent thinking, Stalin had Yakir executed during the Great Purge on 11 June 1937. If he had lived, Yakir would have been one of the most important commanders of the Red Army against the Nazi invasion of 1941–45.

Decorated veterans

Another famous Chinese in the Red Army was Bao Qisan, born in 1887 in Shenyang. He was taken to Russia by an officer of the Tsarist army and lived in the Caucasus, where he studied at a local secondary school. He went to work as a sailor on ocean-going cargo vessels, and became fluent in Russian and English.

Bao was working in a factory in St Petersburg when he joined the Red Army in October 1917. He was appointed commander of a battalion of Chinese who fought with distinction on several fronts in the civil war. In early 1919, during a retreat in the Caucasus region, 350 of his 500 men were killed. After the end of the civil war, the Chinese battalion was disbanded. Bao remained in the army, working on land reconstruction projects. He was decorated with a Red Flag medal for his service and bravery.

The Soviet archives have no records of Bao after 1924. According to some accounts, he was killed in the purges of the 1930s; according to others, he returned to China and died fighting in the anti-Japanese war.

All over Russia are unmarked graves of Chinese who died in the civil war. On the tombstones are written 'graves of unknown martyrs' or 'graves of friendship'.

Next to Lenin's mausoleum in Red Square are the names of two Red Army soldiers, Wang and Zhang, inscribed in marble: 'they sacrificed themselves in 1918'. The history of these two men is unknown.

Soviet secret police

In December 1917, a decree of Vladimir Lenin created the Cheka, the first of a series of Soviet state security organisations. It was led by Felix Dzerzhinsky, an aristocrat who became a Communist, and became an important military and security arm of the new government, the forerunner of the KGB.

The Cheka's troops controlled labour camps; ran the Gulag system; conducted requisitions of food; tortured and executed political opponents; and put down rebellions and riots by workers or peasants and mutinies in the Red Army, which was plagued by desertions.

Chinese volunteers who were especially devoted to the Revolution were allowed to join the Cheka and its various military detachments. In 1919, the Cheka had 700 Chinese members, whom it utilised for the arrest and execution of anti-Soviet soldiers.

In his book *Stalin and His Hangmen*, published in 2004, Donald Rayfield wrote: 'When Russian soldiers refused to carry out executions, Latvians and a Chinese force of 500 men were brought in.' As foreigners, Latvians and Chinese had no personal link to the prisoners and thus were believed to have no sympathy for them.

Beijing backs the White Russians

While the Chinese workers were giving their lives for the Russian Revolution, their government supported the other side.

At the end of 1917, Chinese soldiers occupied the China Eastern Railway in Heilongjiang, disarming the pro-Bolshevik Russians who controlled it. Beijing supported an ad hoc government formed by railway manager General Dmitri Horvath, one of the leaders of the anti-Bolshevik movement in the Far East.

In February 1918, the Allied countries withdrew their embassies from Russia; China followed suit, as it was too dangerous to remain. In March, the Soviet government moved the capital from Petrograd to Moscow, which was safer because it was further inland.

Before they left, China's diplomats gave a certificate of appointment with full powers to represent the interests of the overseas Chinese to Liu Zerong, chairman of the Union of China Workers in Russia (UCWR); in case of need, he could ask the Danish Embassy for help. The Danish consulate became the representative office and the union became the intermediary between the Chinese and Soviet governments.

On 28 September 1918, the British, Japanese, American, French and Italian governments protested to Beijing about the Chinese soldiers fighting for the Bolsheviks. Liu Zhengxiang, China's Foreign Minister and its chief representative at the Versailles talks, wrote to the UCWR, telling it to advise the workers to leave the Red Army.

His appeal fell on deaf ears. The workers had no respect for the diplomats who had led a privileged life in St Petersburg and done little to help them.

The cutting of diplomatic relations by the Beijing government meant that it could have no direct contact with the new Soviet regime. It was a grave decision, given that tens of thousands of its citizens remained stranded in Russia. No other Allied nation had to consider such an enormous human burden.

Saving the workers

With the withdrawal of the Chinese Embassy, the UCWR established a good relationship with the Soviets. The new government was more sympathetic to the stranded workers than the Tsarist regime and worked actively to help them; it also had a high regard for Liu Zerong personally. The government provided 3 000 rubles to the UCWR, and the Railway Ministry allowed the workers to obtain free rail tickets home.

From the spring of 1918, the government issued grain coupons, to save the workers from hunger. It appointed people to sit with them during judicial hearings, and also agreed to Liu's request that Chinese workers have the same wages, working hours, medical care and insurance as Russians.

For its part, the union was in a difficult situation, with only three senior officers left in Petrograd. It was overwhelmed by the number of workers needing its help, who were spread all over an enormous country.

In March 1918, one of the union's officers, Zhu Shaoyang, wrote to colleague Zhang Yongkui: 'During the last year, I have aged a lot, because of the job. In the last years, I have used all my energy on behalf of the workers . . . We cannot leave them behind and let them stay in the vast and constantly unstable land of Russia – unlike that band of people in the consulate, who only care for their own interests.

'Recently, the situation of the workers in Ukraine has been very difficult. They are called Bolsheviks or Bolshevik spies who have been sent from Moscow and Petrograd. At the end of September, the Ukraine government ordered the arrest of all the Chinese workers on its territory. Thanks to our efforts, they were quickly released. The government now allows them to live freely, but they are all out of work. Some know their former bosses, some do not.

'During the cold winter, they do not have the slightest protection. If they set up a new government that declares war on the Soviet government, it will be a severe blow for them. Everyone says that all the Chinese join the Red Army and, according to what the papers often write, they kill everyone. In addition, there are a large number of Chinese PoWs released from German and Austrian camps. Our situation is very serious . . . we cannot meet the demands of each worker.'

Moving left

On 24 December 1918, the UCWR moved into what had been the consulate of the Chinese Embassy. Rather than the flag of the Republic of China, it flew a red flag to symbolise the Chinese worker. The government in Beijing did not protest; it wanted to maintain ties with the new Soviet government and used the association as its representative. The government provided financial support and instructed local governments to do all they could to help the repatriation of China's citizens. Once they had arrived in China, the government offered cheap or subsidised fares from Harbin to Changchun and Dalian, from where they could take boats to their homes in Shandong or Hebei provinces. Through all these efforts, thousands of workers were able to return home.

During 1918, the UCWR became an increasingly political organisation. According to *Pravda*, it had 40 000 to 60 000 members, with branches in many cities all over Russia, from the Black Sea to Khabarovsk and Vladivostok; it attracted not only workers but also traders and craftsmen.

In March 1919, Liu Zerong took part in the first meeting of the Communist International as representative of the overseas Chinese; Lenin established the organisation to export the revolution to India, China, Japan, the Philippines and other countries.

Liu took part in two further meetings and met Lenin in August 1920. He received a letter signed by Lenin himself, instructing all units of the government to help him. As a result, the union's branches all over Russia had the support of the local Bolshevik Party, and at its third annual meeting in June 1921, the union established a Communist Party branch.

Going Home

The Chinese workers who did not join the Red Army were left on their own, struggling to survive in the middle of a civil war that further devastated the Russian economy. From 1917 to 1919, output per head halved, most severely in transport and large-scale industry. In Petrograd, in the spring of 1919, an average worker's daily intake was less than 1 600 calories, half the level before the war. Hundreds of thousands of Russians died from hunger, typhus, typhoid, dysentery and cholera.

Chinese workers with a full-time job were fortunate; the rest made a living as best they could, from odd jobs, begging and crime. The priority was how to get home. The Soviet government favoured their return and wanted to facilitate it; the thousands of vagrant Chinese were seen as a burden on the economy and a potential security threat. However, the government believed that repatriation was China's responsibility; Beijing responded by saying it was the responsibility of the Soviets. The new government said it had no money and asked Beijing to pay; use the Boxer indemnity and let the Russia-Asia Bank provide 100 000 yuan, Beijing replied, and Moscow agreed to consider the idea.

By May 1919, between 30 000 and 40 000 Chinese had made it home, thanks to the efforts of the new government. When fighting in the civil war cut the Trans-Siberian Railway, making the journey impossible, the government tried to find jobs for those who remained in Russia.

Thank the British

It was thanks to the British navy that some of the Chinese workers were able to return home. Among them were members of Chinese communities in the Arctic ports of Murmansk and Arkhangelsk, who had earlier worked on the railway from Murmansk to Petrograd. British naval vessels arrived at the ports in the summer of 1918, as part of an intervention by the Allies in northern Russia to support the White Russian forces and prevent stocks of war materiel from falling into the hands of the Bolsheviks or the Germans. The British offered a passage out to those who could pay. A total of sixty Chinese took up the offer, out of a volunteer battalion of 219 who had been fighting for the White Russian army and building defensive fortifications. The vessels took the workers to Britain, from where they returned home via Canada or France. When the Red Army occupied Murmansk in 1920, they found 245 Chinese waiting to travel home.

In November 1919, Zhu Shaoyang, a senior UCWR official, received approval from the Chinese Embassy in Paris to go to southern Russia to help his compatriots there. He first went to France, Italy and Turkey to meet Chinese businessmen and ask for their help in the evacuation. In Turkey, he found 200 workers who had been working in Baku, a major oil-producing city on the Caspian Sea. He arranged for them to work in a mine, while he arranged a ship for them. When their contractor stole most of their pay, the workers went on strike. With the help of the British and Danish ambassadors, Zhu organised another job for the workers in a British-owned factory; the Chinese kept half of their pay, while the other half was placed in a safe in the Danish Embassy to cover their fare home. Zhu was able to raise 456 pounds from four Chinese businessmen towards the cost of the fares. Since the French and Italian navies had already returned home, it fell to the British navy to carry out the evacuation.

Next, Zhu travelled to southern Russia, where more than 10 000 Chinese workers were waiting to leave. He could not accurately estimate the total, as some of the men had been killed fighting for the Red Army and others had died of illness or starvation in the chaos of the civil war. He was able to arrange the evacuation of 271 men on a British boat that was leaving for Turkey. When the Red Army occupied Odessa in February 1920, the British left and Zhu went with them; it was the end of his mission.

Vladivostok

Among Russian cities with a Chinese population, Vladivostok was exceptional. In 1917, 30 per cent of its population of 97 000 were Chinese. While many were migrant labourers, others had substantial businesses, including shops, factories and large properties; they ran restaurants, bakeries and laundries. In the centre of the city today is a remarkable labyrinth of narrow passageways, houses, yards and staircases. This is where the Chinese once lived.

In late 1917, a Bolshevik administration took over the city, led by a university student named Konstantin Sukhanov and backed by a majority of the local soviet of deputies representing workers, sailors and soldiers. Like businesspeople all over Russia, the Chinese were alarmed by the Revolution and what it would mean for them.

When the new administration began taking over the city's factories and military facilities, the Chinese Chamber of Commerce appealed to their government for help, as did the chambers of Heihe River,

Khabarovsk and Amur province. They proposed that the government send soldiers to cities close to the border, and they also appealed to the two most powerful warlords in Manchuria, Sun Liechen and Zhang Zuolin. The Chinese consul in Vladivostok supported these appeals.

On 13 March 1918, the government took the decision to send a commercial ship, the *Flying Whale*, and its largest naval vessel, the *Hai Rong*. The *Hai Rong* set out on 9 April and arrived in Vladivostok a week later to a warm welcome by the Chinese community. It was the first time the Chinese government had used ships to evacuate its citizens from a foreign country.

When the city government refused permission for two coffins to be brought on board the *Flying Whale*, the *Hai Rong* sent forty soldiers to escort them, and the government backed down. On 18 April, the *Flying Whale* left Vladivostok with 1 165 Chinese on board, headed for the port of Yantai in Shandong. The *Hai Rong* sent soldiers to Vladivostok on several occasions, to protect Chinese who had been surrounded by Russian workers, angered by the competition for jobs.

The Allies were closely watching Vladivostok, where 650 000 tonnes of war materiel they had provided was stockpiled on the wharves. Eager to keep this strategic port out of the control of the Red Army, the Allies decided to intervene in the Russian Far East and support a White Russian government that would continue the war against Germany.

In June 1918, Allied marines landed from warships in Golden Horn Bay. Seizing the railway station, arsenal and other strategic places, they toppled the local soviet, arrested Sukhanov and took control of the Allies' war materiel. By the end of July, a White Russian administration led by General Dmitri Horvath had taken over the city's administrative, judicial and financial functions. More than 20000 local residents took part in a 'funeral' to mark the 'fall' of the city.

In August 1918, an Allied intervention force of 90000 troops arrived in Siberia. Of these, 70000 were Japanese and 8000 were American, along with 4000 Canadians, 4000 Chinese, 2400 Italians, 1500 British, 800 French and several thousand Poles. Japan had been the only Allied power not to send soldiers to the front in France and Belgium; now, it was the only country with a large number of troops ready for such an operation.

By November, the Japanese had occupied all ports and major towns in the Maritime Province and in Siberia east of Chita. The Japanese government and military hated Communism; if they could not prevent the Soviets taking power, they wanted at least to create a pro-Western buffer state in Siberia.

The Chinese government decided to join the

operation, and for the first time in the modern era it sent a military force outside its own borders. The aim was to protect its citizens in Russia, safeguard its interests on the Amur River and take back the land seized by the Tsarist government. On 22 August, 4000 of its soldiers, including cavalry, infantrymen, artillery and machine gun battalions, entered Siberia. In some towns, the soldiers found no Russian police or military presence, and that resident Chinese had armed themselves for their own protection.

The Allied intervention failed in the summer of 1919. The White regime in Siberia collapsed, after the Red Army captured and executed its leader, Admiral Aleksander Kolchak. A former commander of the Black Sea Fleet under the Tsar, he had set up a 'national government' in Omsk, the capital of Siberia. In June 1920, the Americans, British and other Allied soldiers withdrew from Vladivostok. The Japanese did not withdraw until October 1922; they lost a total of 5000 men from combat or illness and the expedition cost over 900 million yen.

In November 1920, the Soviet government set up the Far East province and made the purchase and sale of grain a state monopoly. When the Red Army captured Vladivostok on 25 October 1922, the Russian civil war finally came to an end.

The new government did not like the Chinese

business community; it suspected the Chinese of hoarding and speculation, and was wary of their close relationship with the government in Beijing. The Soviet government began to implement nationalisation and a ban on private business. There would be no place for Chinese factory owners, launderettes, bakers and restaurants in the new workers' state. Most of the businessmen left for home, leaving their homes, factories and businesses behind.

Bitter return

For many workers, the return to China had been a dramatic odyssey, involving months of waiting, hiding, broken journeys, begging and fear. They left behind many friends and colleagues who would never return home.

When they finally crossed the border into China, they expected a warm welcome – but they did not receive it. Instead, the government regarded them with suspicion.

Many of the workers had fought in the Red Army or joined other Bolshevik organisations, and it was feared that they would be used by the Soviet government to spread Communism. Lenin talked of world revolution and spreading his philosophy outside the borders of Russia: were these men to be his tools to incite the workers and farmers of China to overthrow their masters and introduce socialism? Beijing demanded that local authorities keep the workers under surveillance. Zhang Zuolin, the most powerful warlord of Manchuria, ordered that returnees be questioned and urged to move on to their original homes. Some were detained; a few were refused entry into China.

About 40 000 returnees settled in Harbin, the most Russian city in China. After the Revolution, more than 100 000 Russians from the White armies and other refugees fled Harbin, and it became the largest Russian city outside the Soviet Union. The city had a Russian school system and published Russian newspapers and journals. It was an international metropolis, with consulates from sixteen countries, Christian churches of many denominations and fifty-three nationalities speaking forty-five languages. It was an industrial, commercial and banking centre, where the returnees could find work. Financially, they had to start from zero, as the rubles they had in their pockets were worthless and could not be exchanged.

Turning red

The suspicions of the Beijing government were not unfounded. The workers had lived through one of the most extraordinary events in history – the transformation of an absolute monarchy into the world's first Communist state. Many had risked their lives as soldiers to make the Revolution succeed.

In their own country, a revolution had also over-thrown an ancient imperial system and replaced it with a republic. But this revolution had left in place many of the pieces of the empire – the system of land tenure, private business and the privileged status of foreign companies and individuals. The central government was weak and inefficient: warlords controlled large regions of the country. The lives of millions of Chinese were no better after the revolution than before.

The Soviet revolution had great appeal for many Chinese; they saw how a revolt of the poor and the working class had replaced a feudal monarchy and had succeeded in defending it against the might of Japan, Britain, France and other colonial powers.

They saw the terrible slaughter of World War One, which killed nearly ten million soldiers and devastated large areas of Europe. They saw the motives for the war – the national interests of the belligerents – and how the peace settlement had left the winners – especially Britain, France, Japan and the United States – more powerful than they had been before.

What benefits did the victory bring China, Egypt, India and the French and British colonies in Africa that had contributed tens of thousands of men and enor-mous quantities of war materiel? Their sacrifice had not brought independence for these countries or improved rights for their people. Did the principles of democracy and self-determination that President Woodrow Wilson had outlined in his famous speech of 8 January 1918 only apply to countries whose people were European?

Under the Versailles Peace Treaty, China had not succeeded in winning back the part of its own territory of Shandong that had been occupied by Germany and seized by Japan in 1914. The war, it seemed, had not improved the justice or morality of the international order. For many Chinese, Russia's revolution offered the hope of both improving the conditions of the poor and underprivileged at home and introducing a fairer world order.

In July 1919, the Russian deputy commissar for foreign affairs, L. M. Karakhan, announced that the new government would reject the past policies of Tsarist imperialism: it would relinquish its special rights in Manchuria, cancel all former Tsarist secret treaties with China, Japan and the European powers, renounce all further indemnities due from the Boxer Uprising and return the Chinese Eastern Railway to China without compensation.

The Soviet goal was 'to free the people from the yoke of the military force of foreign money which is crushing the people of the East and principally the people of China'. This would have meant returning to China one million square kilometres of the Far Eastern region, including Vladivostok and Khabarovsk. His words moved and inspired many Chinese and made them believe that the regime in Moscow was a better and more moral government.

But the offer was not formalised into a treaty. Lenin died in January 1924 and his successor, Josef Stalin, never repeated the offer; his actions were similar to those of the nationalist leaders of the colonial countries. The Soviet Union and Russia would never have such a Sinophile leader as Lenin again.

Qu Qiubai

Although the workers who returned to China did not play a direct role in founding the Chinese Communist Party (CCP) in July 1921, many brought back with them an admiration of what they had seen and experienced in Russia, knowledge of the Russian language, culture and way of thinking, and contacts with people in the Soviet Union. They would make an important contribution to the growth of the new ideology in China.

Among the leaders of the CCP, the person with the most direct experience of the Soviet Union was Qu Qiubai. Born in January 1899 into a wealthy family that had fallen on hard times, Qu was an intellectual who studied Buddhism, classical Chinese and the works of Bertrand Russell. In the spring of 1917, after failing to pass the civil service exam, he studied Russian at a language institute of the Ministry of Foreign Affairs.

He first encountered Marxism at meetings hosted at Beijing University by its head librarian, Li Dazhao; it was at these meetings that he met Mao Zedong, who would become the first leader of Communist China in 1949.

In 1920 Qu was sent to Moscow as a correspondent for Beijing's *Morning News*. Life was harsh in Russia but he was uplifted by what he saw as the nobility of the Russian character.

'Now I am happy, for I have seen the lighthouse of the mind's sea,' he wrote in one report. 'Even though it is but a single red ray, weak and indistinct, it is possible to see in it the approaching infinite progress.'

He heard Lenin speak, talked with a senior commissar about 'proletarianised education' and walked around Yasnaya Polyana, the estate of Leo Tolstoy, with the great man's grand-daughter Sofya. In early 1922, he joined the Soviet Communist Party.

In January 1922, Qu was one of the interpreters for a meeting of 'Toilers of the Far East' in Moscow, attended by representatives from China, Mongolia, Korea, Japan, Java and India. Grigory Zinoviev, spokesman of the Comintern, told them: 'Remember that the process of history has placed the question thus. You either win your independence side by side with the proletariat or you do not win it at all. Either you receive your emancipation at the hands of the proletariat, in co-operation with it and under its guidance, or you are doomed to remain the slaves of an English, American and Japanese camarilla (courtier).'

In January 1923, Qu accepted an invitation from Chen Duxiu, then leader of China's Communist Party, to return from Russia; he became responsible for the party's propaganda work. In 1927, after the fall of Chen, he became de facto leader of the party. He translated the official Chinese version of the Internationale, which became the CCP's anthem.

In April 1928, he returned to Moscow and stayed for two years as the CCP's representative. In 1930, he was dismissed from the party leadership during intense arguments about the means by which the revolution should be carried out.

Qu was executed by Nationalist soldiers on 18 June 1935 in Changting, Fujian province.

Return to Russia

Russian government companies stopped recruiting Chinese after the October Revolution, though private firms continued to do so until 1922, particularly for projects in Siberia. The new Soviet state did not require Chinese investors or entrepreneurs, but it still needed labour for the Far East. During the first Five Year Plan (1928–32), the Soviet Union imported many workers into the region, to work in ports, factories, forestry, inland transport and laundries.

The Soviet government used the Chinese to develop and move cargoes at the port of Vladivostok. The workers were also employed in gold mines in the Amur region; between 800 and 1000 Chinese labourers were hired in 1928. These workers were at the bottom of the social ladder, just as they had been during World War One. They were given one month's holiday a year, and received evening classes in socialism and were encouraged to take the ideology back to China.

The 1926 census found 100000 Chinese still in the Soviet Union, of whom 70000 were in the Far East. However, the situation was changing. Stalin had forgotten Lenin's internationalist outlook and his promises to treat the workers of the world equally, and had introduced xenophobic policies. On 5 January 1926, the government's Foreign Affairs Committee announced measures to prevent Chinese and Koreans from entering Russia, saying that they presented a 'serious danger'.

During the Great Purges of the 1930s, the Chinese were driven out of Russia. Between 1931 to 1934 and 1937 to 1938, approximately 8000 Chinese were forcibly expelled and more than 10000 arrested. The last group of men was deported in 1938.

The government encouraged or forced Russians to move to the Far East to replace the Chinese workers. The contribution of the Chinese was struck from the history books, which were rewritten to state that it was only the Russians who had developed the region.

By the 1940s, for the first time in 100 years, there were no Chinese in the Far East region. As the centre of the Soviet Pacific Fleet, Vladivostok was closed to foreigners and the only city in the Pacific Rim without a Chinatown.

It was only after the break up of the Soviet Union in 1991, following an absence of fifty years, that the Chinese returned to Vladivostok and the Russian Far East, as workers and investors.

ACKNOWLEDGEMENTS

In writing this book, I would like to thank many people, especially the scholars from China, Taiwan, Russia and Britain who have carried out detailed research on the topics covered in these chapters. Given the nature of the subject matter, this research was very challenging. I salute them for their determination and hard work.

These scholars include Li Yongchang, author of *Chinese Workers in Russia and the October Revolution*, one of the most detailed works on the subject. Also Chen Sanching of the Institute of Modern History, Academica Sinica, in Taipei; He Ping, professor of history at Soochow University in Taiwan; Liu Tao, professor at Yanbian University, Jilin province; and Bu Junzhe of the Beijing Haidian Foreign Language School.

I would also like to thank Bertil Lintner for his excellent *World.Wide.Web* and his work on the Chinese workers in the Russian Far East. Also Zhang Yan of the history department of Shandong University and Yip Siu-jun, a journalist in Hong Kong, for their assistance in providing contacts and material.

Another important source was *Russia's Home Front 1914–1922: The Economy* by Mark Harrison and Andrei Markevich.

The Penguin China Specials:
First World War Series

The First World War may well have been the twentieth century's most significant event, its myriad ripple effects and consequences are still being felt today. However, to date, it has mostly been seen from a European perspective, images of brave, young soldiers in the trenches have, quite rightly, been seared deep on the collective consciousness of the West and their sacrifice should never be forgotten. That said, as with most things in life, the war was far more complex than that and it led – both directly and indirectly – to the Bolshevik Revolution in Russia, the May Fourth Movement in China and Japanese imperialism in the Far East, as well as, of course, the Second World War and its resulting Cold War. To mark its centenary Penguin is publishing a series of Specials which will look at the conflict from a different perspective.

If you enjoyed this Penguin China Special why not try another in the First World War series:

The Siege of Tsingtao: The only battle of the First World War to be fought in Asia by Jonathan Fenby

The Chinese Labour Corps: The Forgotten Chinese Labourers of the First World War by Mark O'Neill

Betrayal in Paris: How the Treaty of Versailles Led to China's Long Revolution by Paul French

Getting Stuck in for Shanghai by Robert Bickers

From the Tsar's Railway to the Red Army: The Experience of Chinese Labourers in Russia During the First World War and Bolshevik Revolution by Mark O'Neill

Picnics Prohibited: China in the First World War by Frances Wood

England's Yellow Peril: Sinophobia and the Great War by Anne Witchard